The Church in Mission

WILBERT R. SHENK

HERALD PRESS
Scottdale, Pennsylvania
Kitchener, Ontario

THE CHURCH IN MISSION

Published by Herald Press, Scottdale, Pa. 15683
Released simultaneously in Canada by Herald Press,
Kitchener, Ont. N2G 4M5
Library of Congress Catalog Card Number: 84-81231
International Standard Book Number: 0-8361-3377-3
Printed in the United States of America
Design by Alice B. Shetler/Art by Joseph Alderfer

90 89 88 87 86 85 84 10 9 8 7 6 5 4 3 2 1

Distributed overseas by Mennonite Board of Missions,
1251 Virginia Avenue, Harrisonburg, Va. 22801-2497.

CONTENTS

PREFACE

The word *mission* has various meanings: task, work, calling, assignment, ministry—to name a few.

The author notes that mission begins with the nature and purpose of God. God is the Creator. God is love. God forgives and saves from sin. God makes whole. This is God's nature and mission.

The Bible defines mission by showing God acting out love, care, and redemption for a fallen creation. Later the church became an agent for carrying out God's mission of love to the world.

In this booklet the author presents a well-rounded, biblical base for the mission of the church. He shows how Christian mission is rooted in the Old Testament, points to Christ as the source of energy for mission, and notes that the Holy Spirit empowers Christians for witness.

The author writes as one who has lived, studied, and experienced missions for some thirty years. Several questions at the end of each chapter help to pinpoint important truths and make personal applications.

The Church in Mission is volume 15 in the Mennonite Faith Series listed inside the back cover. To pursue the theme further, check the references placed at the back of the book.

—*J. Allen Brubaker*

1

THE STARTING POINT

THE words *mission, missions,* and *missionary* have become so much a part of Christian vocabulary that we may overlook an important fact: the Bible does not use these words. As we read early church history, though, we are struck by the sense of mission which marked those first disciples.

Instead of giving us a word for mission, the Bible pictures the young church in action. Certain people were called and set apart to take the news about Jesus Christ to peoples who had not yet heard this news. Other believers simply and naturally witnessed to their neighbors in Jerusalem or Antioch. And wherever the believers went the church grew.

Among the religions of the world one finds few examples of such missionary consciousness. By "missionary consciousness" we mean that a religious group feels compelled by the inner force of its faith to share that faith so that others accept it as their own. Most religions are closely tied to a particular clan or tribe of people. This type of tribal religion arises out of its own history and is suited to its needs. Such a faith is therefore not intended to be shared with outsiders.

Biblical faith challenges that limited understanding of religion. Some Jewish groups began to think and act in missionary ways during periods of exile before the time of Christ. Jesus denounced the scribes and Pharisees for the way they carried on their missionary activity (Matthew 23:15). But early in his ministry Jesus began to send his disciples on preaching missions. He sent them to announce what God was doing in the world and to invite men and women to turn to God with all their hearts.

Of all religions, only those serving one God— Judaism, Christianity, and Islam—have had a missionary consciousness. These three faiths have had quite different understandings as to the meaning of their mission to the world and how it is to be carried out. Mission is at the heart of biblical faith. Our purpose here is to develop a sketch of mission.

Some Understandings of Mission

Christians have not always agreed on the starting point or foundation of mission. Several ideas have played an important role in the thinking of Christians concerning mission at various times in history. Each has merit, but none gives a complete picture of the whole purpose of mission.

1. *Mission is based on a command of Jesus.* The Great Commission, especially as found in Matthew 28:19-20, has often been read as a command to mission. This idea received special emphasis when William Carey published a book in 1792 entitled *An Inquiry into the Obligations of Christians to Use Means for the Conversion of the Heathens.* Through this book Carey sought to arouse the Christian church to its missionary responsibility. He based his appeal firmly on the Great Commission. As a result, the modern missionary movement, which dates from about 1792, drew much of its inspiration from the Great Commission.

Such an emphasis is noticeably absent from the Epistles. The Great Commission does not stand alone, rather, it must be seen in relation to Pentecost (Acts 1:8).

2. *Mission is an important element in the nature of the church.* The church has several tasks. Among these is that of witnessing to the world. The church is also responsible to nurture its own members, do deeds of charity, and maintain a life of worship and fellowship. At any given moment the church may give less attention to one of these tasks while another is given more attention. Some of these tasks may become dormant while the church concerns itself with what it considers most urgent at the time. While the several tasks remain the work of the church, each will be expressed as the church feels led.

3. *Mission is a way of relieving some of the immense needs of the world.* It is sometimes suggested that we can justify missionary activity to the extent

it helps to meet human need. These needs are to be found everywhere, but especially among the poorer nations. Efforts to reduce human suffering can always be justified, but particularly as an expression of the love of God in Christ.

4. *Mission serves the economic and political needs of the nation from which missionaries are sent.* We usually associate this missionary motive with earlier periods of history. For example, in the late fifteenth and early sixteenth centuries the Spanish and Portuguese kings were authorized by the pope to "convert the heathen." They did this as a part of their economic and political expansion into other parts of the world. In the nineteenth century when the leading European powers established colonies in Asia and Africa, some people felt that missions were a necessary part of the process. They felt that missions could play an important role in establishing government over the peoples being colonized.

But even in the nineteenth century this motive for mission was seen to be a two-edged sword. People who were being ruled by a colonial power generally opposed attempts to force them to accept the religion of their conquerors.

5. *Mission is a means of correcting past wrongs.* Especially in the nineteenth century some people argued that the Christians of Europe were responsible to share the gospel with the peoples of Asia and Africa to atone for the wrongs the Europeans had done to these nations. For example, appeals were made to send missionaries to Africa in order to pay for the terrible crime committed against the African peoples by white slave traders. Missionaries and

their home boards got involved in efforts to stop the slave trade, introduce education, and restore dignity to the African peoples.

Each of these motives for mission has some merit. Yet each one is inadequate and cannot stand alone. We need to search further for our answer.

Starting Point: God

We will arrive at a biblical understanding of mission only if we attempt to see it through the eyes of God. Let's examine God's purpose and plan.

1. *God is love and loves the world* (John 3:16, 17). The Bible pictures for us a God who never gives up and never lets go of humankind. At the center of human history stands the supreme expression of God's love, the cross. In the sacrifice of Jesus Christ on the cross for the salvation of humankind, we see God in mission.

2. *God created the world and humankind* (Genesis 1, 2; John 1:4). God's action in creating the world and human beings was already an expression of love. The created world and the place of the human family in it were perfect. There was perfect harmony between God and creation.

3. *God has a plan for humankind.* When Adam and Eve fell into sin, they thereby corrupted themselves and brought disorder into the world (Genesis 3). The human fall introduced a new element into the picture. Disharmony now marks the relationship between human beings and between humans and nature. Cain killed his brother Abel and then lived with a curse on his life the rest of his days (Genesis 4:1-16). The earth also began producing thorns and thistles.

4. *God takes new action.* Because sin came into the human race, God has taken many new initiatives. In the flood, God preserved Noah and his family in order to provide a new beginning for the human family. God made a covenant with Abraham, promising that through him and his descendants the rest of the world would be blessed. Through Moses God delivered the children of Israel out of Egypt, gave them the law at Sinai, and restored them to the Promised Land. God sent prophets and allowed Israel to have the king they demanded. Yet each of these steps was not enough.

5. *God's final plan: God comes personally* (Isaiah 43; Ezekiel 36:16-32; John 1:14, 17, 18; 1 John 4:9f.; Ephesians 1:3-14; Colossians 1:15-20; Revelation 5:9-14; 7:9-12). God expressed divine love for the world finally and perfectly by coming personally to redeem the world. The system of ritual sacrifice under the law of Moses gives us some clues to the meaning of God's perfect sacrifice. When God wanted to test Abraham's commitment, God commanded Abraham to sacrifice his beloved son Isaac on the altar. When God saw the genuineness of Abraham's commitment, God intervened and provided "the lamb for the burnt offering" (Genesis 22:8). Abraham's words anticipated Christ who became that "burnt offering" which God personally provided. The action of Jesus Christ replaced the old system of animal sacrifices.

6. *Every initiative has been God's.* All we know of mission we see in God's words and actions (John 1:14). The testimony of all Scripture is that God has always been seeking and saving people. Before we knew God, God knew us. Before we sought God,

God sought us. Before we found God, God found us. Before we loved God, God loved us. God's heart is a missionary heart. This is the God who sent the Son and in turn sends us.

All genuine missionary activity reflects God's mission

For the church there can be only one mission. That mission is the one revealed to us in God's actions described above: God's mission is to "bring all things in Christ . . . to the praise of his glory" (Ephesians 1:10, 14) by forming a new people and ultimately a new heaven and a new earth. Every activity which we call mission can be authentic only to the degree it reflects God's mission.

We will keep this distinction clearer if we contrast *mission* and *missions*.

In the natural world, the sun is the center of the universe because it is the sole source of energy. For example, the moon, as it circles around the earth, gives off a certain amount of light. That light, however, is not generated by the moon but is rather sun energy reflected from the moon to earth.

This example from the physical universe is an illustration of the relationship between God and his people. God stands at the center of our universe. The mission is God's mission—as described in the previous section—and results from divine energy.

We are like so many little moons orbiting around the universe reflecting some part of the light of God. These little moons are like the specific initiatives or *missions* in which we engage out of obedience to our missionary God. These missions are always imperfect reflections of the great mission. They are often marked by failures of vision and commitment. To the extent that some light from God is transmitted, they are faithful channels of God's mission.

Questions

1. State in your own words the mission of God.
2. What has motivated you, your church, and your denomination to engage in missions?
3. What specific missions are you involved in? How are those a part of God's mission?

2

OLD TESTAMENT ROOTS

CHRISTIAN mission is rooted in the Old Testament. In Genesis 1-3 we can identify at least nine themes which set the pattern of salvation history.[*]

1. *God is initiator.* Genesis begins: "In the beginning God created . . ." (1:1a). God stands over and beyond the material world. God is not limited by time and space. God acts on behalf of creation.

2. *As Creator, God also controls.* The universe is God's by right of creation. God has not abandoned

[*]Adapted from Richard R. DeRidder, "The Old Testament Roots of Mission," in Wilbert R. Shenk (ed.) *Exploring Church Growth* (Eerdmans, 1983, pp. 173-175).

the world to some other power. God rules the universe.

3. *God calls the creation good.* God repeatedly pronounced the creation work "good." This allows for no rejection of the world. The world remains the object of God's loving concern.

4. *God makes men and women caretakers or stewards of the created world.* God made people in the divine image. Thus humankind has intelligence, wisdom, and the ability to care for the creation in line with God's intentions.

5. *God makes a unity of all humankind.* Genesis 1-3 speaks of humankind as a unity: "male and female he created them." All human beings have one origin, one purpose, one goal, with no distinction except that of male and female.

6. *Satan represents those forces which oppose God.* At the suggestion of the serpent—who stands for evil—man and woman disobeyed God (Genesis 3). This spiritual warfare has marked human existence ever since. All spirits are described as being subject to God, even those which are evil and in rebellion.

7. *Despite the human fall, God still rules over all creation.* God does not deviate from the divine purpose or surrender control over the universe (Ephesians 1:3-14; Colossians 1:3-20).

8. *God's concern includes the entire human family* (Matthew 28:18-20; Acts 1:8; Romans 1:14-16).

9. *God's claim and call remain in force despite the fall.* Although humankind received judgment in being sent out of Eden, God sent Adam and Eve out with a mission—"to work the ground from which

[they] had been taken" (Genesis 3:23). God did not cut off relationship with them. They were to continue as caretakers of the earth.

Tension Between Human and Divine

Genesis 3 shows how humankind became rebellious against God. This tension between God's will and human willfulness is a theme throughout the Bible. The elements of this tension include:

human rebellion/pride	divine grace/love
human sinfulness	divine righteousness
human unfaithfulness, e.g., covenant breaking	divine faithfulness, e.g. covenant keeping

This tension is graphically pictured for us in the story of the Tower of Babel (Genesis 11:1-9). The people of Shinar set out to build a city. It included "a tower that reaches to the heavens, so that we may make a name for ourselves. . . ."

The people in the story clearly expressed their rebellious pride against God's intention for them. They went beyond God's purposes. Indeed, they attempted to become like God, intending to build a tower that would enable them to escape the limits of time and space. Instead of seeking to find their fulfillment in fellowship with God, they expressed their spirit of independence. Through their actions they brought God's judgment on themselves. Thereafter they suffered confused communication and broken relationships which trouble humankind to this day.

The point of the story is clear: When human beings insist on following their own wisdom and designs, they experience confusion and brokenness.

Only by accepting God's way and being restored to harmony with God are we also reconciled to one another and to God's created world.

Call of Abraham

The people of Babel had arrogantly asserted: ". . . let us . . . make a name for ourselves" (Genesis 11:4). Immediately following the story of Babel the Bible tells of God's call to one man, Abram (later called Abraham). God responds to Babel with a new offer. God promises: "I will make you into a great nation and I will bless you; I will make your name great, and you will be a blessing" (Genesis 12:2).

Abraham and his descendants thus are elected and enter into a new covenant with God. This is called the universal covenant because God has in view "all the families of the earth." God never stopped loving the whole created world. God longed to reveal to all peoples divine love and mercy. Thus God chose Abraham and his family to be the means of blessing and salvation, but not because they possessed prestige or power. On the contrary, in the eyes of the world they were insignificant.

God's election of Israel and covenant with them are expressions of divine grace toward Abraham and all peoples. Abraham cannot, therefore, view his call as based on personal merit. Rather, it is simply because God has singled him out to perform a special mission for the salvation of the whole world.

Creation of People of God: Exodus and Sinai

The Scriptures make clear that when God called Abraham and his tribe to their special role in the history of salvation, God did not choose them because of any special qualifications. Rather, the Scriptures emphasize their modest background, even their insignificance. They brought to this role no financial, political, or economic power.

Abraham lived among peoples who worshiped the sun, moon, and various other gods. But God broke through to Abraham and his descendants with a clear revelation. God stands over creation and now invites this people to fulfill a special role in the story of salvation. God promised to make of them a new kind of people.

The exodus and Sinai experiences powerfully formed Israel's sense of peoplehood. The people of Israel, in the midst of desperate famine conditions, had gone into Egypt. There they fell into slavery and were severely exploited by the Egyptians. Eventually God raised up Moses as the leader who led the people of Israel in their deliverance from Egypt. Soon after the exodus from Egypt, at Sinai, God gave to Moses the Ten Words, the new law by which the people were to live. Exodus and Sinai represent the two roots of identity for the people of God in the Old Testament.

As a part of that identity, the people of Israel knew that they were called, as was Abraham, to bring blessing to the world. The God they served was not a tribal deity. Rather, the people of Israel proclaimed before the world that one God is Lord of all peoples. This God directs all of history and reunites all peoples (Exodus 20; Psalm 24:1).

Because God was sovereign over all people, Israel invited all to acclaim Jahweh as their God also (Psalm 67).

Israel as the people of God, therefore, lived in the

hope that all peoples would ultimately gather with them in united worship of the one true God. Thus God chose a particular people to bring this message to the whole world; but the message they carried was an invitation for all peoples to return to the God who was both their Creator and Redeemer.

Messianic Prophecies: Expectation of God's Continuing Action

God's people did not remain faithful to the covenant. They lived through repeated cycles of revival and apostasy. The revivals of spiritual vitality in the Old Testament owe much to the ministry of the prophets. These prophets announced judgment on the sins of the people and held before them a vision of what God wanted to do in their lives and in the future.

These messianic prophecies anticipated God's continuing initiative. The message of the prophets centered on the coming of God's Messiah who would establish an entirely new order. In this new kingdom God's people would serve with singleness of heart. Their relationships would be based on justice and righteousness, and every individual would be restored to all that God had intended in the original creation.

1. *The Messiah* (Isaiah 11:1-10). Of all the prophets, Isaiah most clearly described for us the Messiah and the new age. This messianic age, he said, would stand in sharp contrast to the world order. The Messiah would act in totally different ways from the human way. In the book of Isaiah the character of the Messiah is pictured in four ways:

a. *As a meek and lowly deliverer* (Isaiah 42:1-9;

61:1-4). The Messiah is the new Moses, the one who leads the people to liberation in the new exodus. The Spirit of God is upon the Messiah in fullness. He is pictured as a servant, not a powerful ruler.

b. *As the head of redemption* (Isaiah 49:1-13). The Messiah fills the special role of redeemer, the one who calls Israel back to God. He is also "a light to the nations, that my salvation may reach to the ends of the earth" (RSV). As redeemer, the Messiah will help "to restore the land" and restore God's people to life.

c. *As God's representative* (Isaiah 50:4-11; 51:16). The Messiah represents God to the peoples. He bears the scoffing and rejection and faithfully declares God's word, reminding Zion, "You are my people."

d. *As the Lamb of God* (Isaiah 52:13—53:12). The Messiah is the lamb sacrificed on the altar to take away the sins of the people. When Abraham was about to sacrifice Isaac, God intervened and provided a lamb. The prophet sees God the Father offering his son as the perfect and ultimate sacrifice.

2. *The mission of the Messiah.* The Messiah is to gather God's people from the four corners of the world in a great messianic banquet to be held in the new Jerusalem (Isaiah 2:1-4; 18:7; 60:1-3; Jeremiah 16:19; Micah 4:1-4; Zephaniah 3:8-10; Zechariah 8:20-23). The scattering of the peoples following the Tower of Babel will be reversed. The Bible pictures Messiah's work as climaxed by this great feast of celebration.

This indicates clearly that history has purpose and is moving toward a goal. From among the peoples of the world the Messiah seeks and saves those who respond to the Father's invitation to the great feast. The holding of this banquet will mark the completion of time. But the exact schedule for the great feast is known only to God.

Old Testament Pattern of Mission

The Old Testament nowhere gives a clear command to the people of God to go on missions. It is sometimes said that the people of Israel saw themselves as being at the center of God's intentions for the world. They expected that other nations would join them in the worship of God as they themselves were faithful to the covenant. Rather than moving out to the peoples, the Israelites expected the nations to seek out Israel. But already during periods of exile and under the influence of some of the prophets the people of Israel caught some vision of their responsibility to share the great messianic promises with the world.

At times the people of Israel misinterpreted the promise to Abraham. They thought obedience would bring prosperity to them. But from time to time they recovered the original meaning: the people of God were to be the means of blessing other peoples, beyond the benefit this special relationship brought to them.

Although the Old Testament does not contain a clear pattern of mission, all that emerges in the New Testament is clearly rooted in the Old. We cannot understand mission in the New Testament apart from what God has done in and through the people of Israel under the old covenant.

Questions

1. What other Old Testament stories illustrate tension between the human and the divine?
2. What incidents in the Old Testament show how God's chosen people, Israel, shared God's message with others? How did they do it?
3. God called Abraham to be a blessing to all peoples, but Israel interpreted the call as their opportunity to receive God's favor. What do you observe among Christians today? Do they see their call any differently than did Israel?
4. What root experiences shape the sense of peoplehood for Christians?
5. Which pattern of mission does the church employ today: moving out to the world or expecting the world to move toward the church?

3

JESUS CHRIST THE CENTER

AS the story of the Old Testament unfolds, it centers in prophecies concerning the coming Messiah. With great longings the prophets looked forward to a time when Messiah would come and set things right for the people of God and the world. The New Testament continues this emphasis on the Messiah whom God sent to "save his people from their sins." What had been promised under the old covenant was fulfilled under the new.

John the Baptist's singular task was to prepare the people to recognize and receive Jesus as Messiah. He called his hearers to repent because "the kingdom of heaven is near" (Matthew 3:2). John cited Isaiah's words concerning Messiah and his ministry (Isaiah 40:3-5; 52:10) which pointed to a new order of life (Matthew 3:3; Luke 3:4-6). John therefore called people to turn away from their old way of life (repent) and begin living according to Messiah's standards. He gave explicit advice to tax collectors, soldiers, and common folk as to how they might conform their lives to this new way of living (Luke 3:8, 10-14).

The power of his message caused some people to ask whether John himself was the Messiah. John quickly answered that he baptized only with water but the Messiah would baptize "with the Holy Spirit and with fire" (Luke 3:16).

The witness of the early church was that Jesus was indeed the Messiah to whom the prophets had pointed (Acts 2:23-25; 17:1-9; 18:5-6; 26:1-23). Their experiences with Jesus and the new reality he brought to their lives was the basis for their witness.

Jesus Begins His Ministry

1. *Baptism.* The Gospels of Matthew, Mark, and Luke each record the baptism of Jesus. This event marks the transition from private to public figure. At Jesus' baptism, his calling as Messiah was publicly confirmed and his ministry begun.

The Hebrew word *Messiah*—the same word as *Christ* in Greek—means "anointed one," an individual empowered by the Spirit to deliver people from bondage to sin and to establish God's rule. At Jesus' baptism two signs confirmed his messiahship.

a. The Spirit's anointing: "and the Holy Spirit descended on him" (Luke 3:22). This recalls Isaiah's prophecy:

The Spirit of the Lord will rest on him—
the Spirit of wisdom and of understanding,
the Spirit of counsel and of power,
the Spirit of knowledge and of the fear of the Lord.
Isaiah 11:2.

These gifts of the Spirit—wisdom, understanding, power, knowledge, and fear of the Lord—become the means of a new kind of government based on *righteousness* (Isaiah 11:4-5). This "Root of Jesse" will be a sign of God's saving concern for all peoples, including the people of Israel who are not walking in his will (Isaiah 11:10, 11).

b. The voice of confirmation: "This is my Son, whom I love" (Matthew 3:17). These words come from Psalm 2:7 and seem to allude to Isaiah 42:1. Psalm 2 is a royal psalm which describes the rebellion of earthly powers against God and "his anointed." Isaiah 42:1 speaks of "my servant . . . my chosen . . . I will put my Spirit on him and he will bring justice to the nations." This suffering servant is to be the instrument of righteousness and justice precisely because he has rejected the world's way of violence, injustice, and oppression. He becomes the pioneer of our salvation because he acts entirely in accord with the will of God.

2. *Temptations*. Matthew, Mark, and Luke link the baptism and temptations of Jesus. "Immediately," says Mark, following his baptism Jesus went into the wilderness where he faced the devil. The point of the temptations was not that Jesus should not rule. On the contrary, the devil held before him the prospect of great power. If Jesus had accepted the devil's proposal he would have been saying no to the call to be suffering servant. He

would have been rejecting the Father. This Jesus refused to do.

3. *Message.* Jesus could have given no more eloquent and emphatic reply to the devil than the message with which he began his public ministry. His theme was: "Repent, for the kingdom of heaven is near" (Matthew 4:17; cf. Mark 1:15). Rather than sidestepping the issue of power and authority, Jesus faced it directly. He put first the the kingship of God over the realm of Satan. Jesus urged people to repent, to turn around and leave the ways of the world where life is lived under the rule of the devil. Jesus could not accomplish his mission by using political means however. People of Jesus' day could not understand him because he rejected the usual path to power. His calling was to follow the "politics of God."

Jesus' whole message and ministry is based on the kingdom of God. The English word *kingdom* is not the best translation for our purposes. Many people think of a geographical territory where people are governed by a king or queen. However, as used in the Gospels, the word means kingship or rulership. When Jesus announced the gospel of the kingdom, he was inviting men and women to submit their lives to God, allowing God to be ruler of their lives.

The gospel of the kingdom has both a present and a future dimension. Jesus was emphatic: "The kingdom is at hand." It is invading history now. God is taking the initiative to begin the new age by inviting men and women to live under divine rule. Furthermore, God has sent the Son as the personal embodiment of the kingdom; Christ demonstrated before the world divine love, mercy, and righteousness. Thus God acts in Jesus Christ to make the kingdom a present reality.

But the call to accept God's rule is also an invitation to a new future. The kingdom of God has broken into history in the first coming of Jesus Christ, yet Christ's work is not completed. Evil forces are still at work in the world; the foe has not been completely vanquished. The people of God await Christ's coming again when the kingdom of God in all its fullness is manifested. The cry of the church throughout the ages has been, *Maranatha! (Our Lord, come!)*

Neither Jesus nor the disciples gave a precise definition for the meaning of kingdom. The term was a common one among the Jewish people, and Jesus' audience had no difficulty with its meaning. That is not to say, however, that it was completely understood. Indeed, many in the crowds who came to hear Jesus were baffled by what Jesus taught and the way he taught it. He assured the disciples that "the secret of the kingdom of God" had been given to them while casual onlookers missed the message (Mark 4:11).

The coming of the kingdom brings tension. On the one hand, those living out the rule of God here and now are reminded daily how incomplete it is. The present is only a foretaste of what is still to come. The believer lives with the longing for the fullness of kingdom reality while also seeking to be faithful to the calling to be ministers of the kingdom in the world. On the other hand, the presence of the kingdom brings judgment. The kingdom confronts every man and woman with a decision: continue to submit to the devil or repent and follow Christ.

The relationship of kingdom and church is a crucial one. Some people have assumed the kingdom and the church are one and the same thing. The New Testament writers distinguish between kingdom and church.

a. *The kingdom creates the church.* Jesus appealed to the people of his day to respond to the kingdom. The church is comprised of those who have repented and been converted. The church is that body of people who acknowledge Jesus as Lord and seek to live out his will. Without the kingdom there is no body of Christ.

b. *The church witnesses to the kingdom.* The church never witnesses to itself. The thrust of apostolic witness to the gospel concerns the self-revelation of God in the life, death, and resurrection of Jesus Christ. Through the work of Christ God is saving those who acknowledge and appropriate that sovereignty in their lives. The witness of the church is to Jesus as Messiah who redeems and reigns.

c. *The church is the instrument of the kingdom.* We have already noted that the church witnesses to the kingdom. But we must make the point more clearly. The church exists for the service of the King. God entered into covenant with Abraham with the promise that Abraham and his descendants would be the means of blessing to all the nations. Under the new covenant the people of God are elected for service. The church is to practice and proclaim God's love as revealed in Jesus the Messiah.

d. *The church acts under authority of the kingdom.* At every point the kingdom is prior to the church. If Jesus Christ is Lord and head of the church, then clearly the church's only authority is that which Jesus entrusts to it. Whenever the church loses sight of this order in relationship, it runs the risk of acting in ways that are contrary to the will of the head of the church. Faithfulness requires that the church always submit itself to the will of Jesus Christ and seek to discern what obedience means in every circumstance.

4. *Sermon on the Mount: Charter for New Peoplehood.* In Matthew's Gospel the Sermon on the Mount comes early in Jesus' ministry. It is placed shortly after he has chosen the twelve disciples and has begun moving about the Galilee region. Matthew 5—7 is highly significant as a missionary statement. The Beatitudes describe pointedly the kind of community the people of God are when they embody kingdom reality. As John Driver states: "If, by God's grace, we are the kind of community described by the Beatitudes, and if, in the power of the Spirit, we live the life described in the Sermon on the Mount, then our presence and proclamation will carry kingdom content. It will season and purify and enlighten relationships within human society."* In other words, the integrity of missionary witness depends on the degree to which the sending community lives out in daily life the vision it proclaims.

One of Jesus' first actions as he began his public ministry was to gather about him twelve disciples—those who would share intimately in the witness. Missionary witness should always lead to the creation of a new community of believers. The presence

---

*John Driver, "Mission: Salt, Light, and Covenant Law," *Mission Focus*, 11:3 (September 1983), p. 33.

of this new community is itself a part of the good news. The gospel of the kingdom has the power to create this new peoplehood. Jesus announced this as *good* news. Men and women can be liberated from the slavery of the old life and enter into a life of freedom. Whereas the old way inevitably leads to death, the way of the kingdom of God goes by way of cross and resurrection to new life.

Jesus Calls and Commissions

As we have already noted, Jesus' announcement about the kingdom of God also contained an invitation. Men and women were urged to claim God's grace for their own lives. But the invitation was also to "follow me." Jesus invested three years in the training of his band of twelve disciples in "followership." As a part of that training Jesus commissioned and sent his disciples on preaching and healing missions several times (Matthew 10; Mark 4:14; Luke 9, 10).

Jesus taught his disciples both the meaning of God's kingdom and the way this was to be worked out in life. He also demonstrated how to witness. His classroom was the street corner or the hillside or the sickroom. His disciples saw him heal the sick, cast out evil spirits, rebuke evil powers, and speak words of grace and forgiveness to sinners. They both received his love and saw him minister compassionately to the poor and oppressed.

Thus Jesus made his mission of preaching, teaching, healing, and confronting evil powers the mission of his disciples. What he had been doing he, in turn, commissioned them to continue (John 17:18; 20:19-23).

Jesus' Mission Leads to Cross

The keynote of Jesus' ministry was the kingdom of God. Without apology Jesus called his hearers to make a break with the old order and join God's way. Thus his message brought judgment on the religious and civil leaders of his day, for they were continuing the old order. The three years of Jesus' public ministry were marked by mounting tension between Jesus and the authorities. Finally they plotted his death and had him crucified.

The word for *witness* early became *martúrion* from which we get the word *martyr*. In other words, for Jesus and the early disciples to be a witness for the kingdom of God involved the risk of death for the sake of the gospel. Witness to the Christian gospel will always be costly when it is genuine and carried out in a Christ-like manner.

Post-Resurrection Commissioning

The Gospel writers note that soon after the resurrection Jesus commissioned his disciples to carry on his ministry. (John reports this happening the evening of resurrection Sunday.) Early in Jesus' ministry he had sent his disciples out on brief missions. Before his ascension he renewed this commission in the light of the resurrection event. Everything was not ready, however. The carrying out of this commission was dependent on their waiting for the final credential—the power of the Holy Spirit fully present and at work in their lives.

Questions

1. How does Jesus Christ fit into God's mission? What did his mission include?
2. Describe God's kingdom and show how the church relates to it.
3. How is the good news of the kingdom being lived and shared in your community?
4. How do you experience the tension between the kingdom having come but not yet having been completed?
5. In what ways have you felt the clash between the kingdom of God and the kingdom of the world?

4

THE HOLY SPIRIT AND MISSION

MESSIAH means *anointed one*. The anointed one was the Spirit-filled representative of God among his people (Isaiah 42:1). The people of Israel knew that the Messiah would be the one filled with the Spirit of God.

Just before his ascension Jesus repeated to his disciples what he had said earlier. He was transferring to them the task the Father had assigned the Son. They were to continue to spread the message about the kingdom of God. The message was to be taken to all peoples, regardless of their race, culture, or politics.

But in preparation for this mission Jesus

instructed the disciples to do one other thing. They were to wait for the coming of the Spirit in their lives. The Spirit was fully present in the Messiah, Jesus. As people of the Messiah, they too were to have the Spirit's power in their lives.

Pentecost

In the yearly cycle of feasts, the people of Israel recalled their exodus from Egypt in the Feast of Passover or Unleavened Bread. Fifty days later they celebrated the giving of the law at Sinai in the Feast of Weeks or Pentecost (Deuteronomy 16:9-12).

Jesus kept the Passover with his disciples on the evening before his arrest, trial, and execution (Matthew 26:1-29). Through the shedding of his blood on the cross Jesus became the lamb of God. Jesus thereby made possible the forgiveness of sin, as symbolized in Passover sacrifice. His triumphant resurrection from the dead assures his followers of release from the powers of death.

Peter in his Pentecostal sermon recorded in Acts 2 tied the New Testament story of salvation to the Old Testament. As Exodus was not complete without Sinai, so the death and resurrection of the Messiah were not complete, in God's purposes, without a new Sinai. In this pouring out of God's Spirit on the people at Pentecost, however, God transformed them by writing the new law on their hearts. Jesus instructed his disciples to wait for this new experience of God's blessing and empowering. Without the Spirit they would be unable to witness to an unbelieving world, for they themselves had not yet experienced the fullness of God's work in their lives.

Acts of the Holy Spirit

Pentecost is one of the most dramatic and decisive events in all of Scripture. God the Spirit came upon the people as they waited expectantly in Jerusalem.

The Spirit's action reversed Babel (Genesis 11:1-9). People "from every nation under heaven" lived in Jerusalem at that time. As word of this event spread through the city, a large crowd gathered. They were bewildered, however, because "each one heard them speaking in his own language. '. . . we hear them telling in our own tongues the mighty works of God' " (Acts 2:6, 11). The rebellion of Babel resulted in a confusion of language and a scattering out of the peoples. Pentecost united peoples of different cultures through hearing "the mighty works of God" and receiving the ministry of God's Spirit in their lives.

Inspired by the Spirit, Peter interpreted the meaning of this event to the assembly. He declared that this fulfilled Joel's prophecy concerning a new pouring out of the Spirit of God. Fresh vision and spiritual manifestations would break forth. This is the day of salvation (Joel 2:28; cf. Isaiah 44:3 and Jeremiah 31:31-34).

What God had promised had now become reality. For a long time the people of Israel had lost sight of God's purpose for them. Now they who believed were seeing with fresh eyes God's purpose and plan for the world. The coming of the Spirit of God confirmed it.

Peter based his interpretation firmly on what God had done in Jesus Christ: his earthly ministry, suffering, death, resurrection, and return to heaven.

The center of Pentecost is Jesus Christ. The ministry of the Holy Spirit is to bear witness to Jesus as God's Messiah, the anointed one.

Pentecost produced a twofold effect. First, every believer was empowered (Acts 2:4). This stands in contrast to the Old Testament age when the Holy Spirit was given only to a few select individuals. The power of the Spirit at Pentecost drew many to faith so that the community of believers grew rapidly.

Second, the church grew out of Pentecost. The church is properly called "the community of the Spirit."* Through the Pentecost event the Spirit created the new Israel. The Spirit created the church for mission, just as God had elected Israel for mission to the nations.

The apostle Paul's teaching on spiritual gifts shows how the church functions as the community of the Spirit (Romans 12:4-8; 1 Corinthians 12; 14; Ephesians 4:7-16). Paul stressed the usefulness of these gifts for mutual growth: "to equip the saints for the work of ministry, for building up the body of Christ" (Ephesians 4:12, RSV).

These gifts operate in two ways. One group of gifts contributes toward meeting the pastoral and nurture needs of the body: teaching, fellowship, pastoral care, mutual aid, discipline, worship. Another group of gifts is given for witness to the world: apostleship, evangelism, prophecy, spiritual discernment. Some gifts serve both the internal as well as external ministries. Balanced body life always includes both the internal and external dimen-

---

*See C. Norman Kraus, *The Community of the Spirit* (Eerdmans, 1974), esp. Chapter 1.

sions. But the church never exists for itself. It exists as a witness to Jesus Christ.

The Witness Spreads

The unfolding story in Acts demonstrates how the Spirit-inspired witness of the apostles affected people. They were transformed by the gospel and filled with the Holy Spirit. These new believers quickly joined the ranks of witnesses. As a result, more and more people became followers of Jesus.

Acts shows us six stages in the development of the church. To help us understand the growth of the early church, we will review briefly these stages. Luke tells the story of each phase by commenting on several elements. He begins with a description of a new thrust in witness. Then he reports the reactions of those who believed and accepted the gospel, as well as reactions against the gospel. Each stage reveals major conflict between the Christian movement and the religious and civil authorities. The Christians often suffered persecution and imprisonment. Luke ends each stage with a summary of the further development of the Christian cause as a result of these confrontations.

1. *Jerusalem (Acts 1:1—6:7).* At first the church was confined largely to Jerusalem, but Luke reports that the church grew by leaps and bounds. This rapid growth brought great stresses and strains. Questions of church leadership had to be worked out under the pressure of rapid growth. Rivalries came to the surface when the Greeks charged the Jews with slighting the Greek widows at the daily food distribution. This need was met by assigning deacons to it.

But even more threatening was the official opposition the new faith aroused. The Jewish high priest ordered the arrest of the apostles. Eventually the authorities released the apostles after beating them and ordering them "not to speak in the name of Jesus" (Acts 5:40).

Luke summarizes this first stage as follows: "So the word of God spread. The number of disciples in Jerusalem increased rapidly, and a large number of priests became obedient to the faith" (Acts 6:7).

2. *To Judea, Galilee, and Samaria (Acts 6:8—9:31).* The account of Stephen's highly successful ministry opens this stage. His success stirred up the fury of synagogue leaders against him. When "they could not withstand the wisdom and the Spirit with which he spoke," they turned to underhanded means—arranging false witnesses and stirring up the people against him. Stephen made a long defense by preaching a sermon on the story of salvation. He ended by charging his accusers with being stiff-necked rebels against the Holy Spirit. Enraged by Stephen's charge, they dragged him out of the city and stoned him. Luke observes that Saul was "giving approval to his death."

Stephen's death unleashed a wave of persecution against the Jerusalem church. As a result of this wave of terror, the Christian community scattered throughout Judea and Samaria. The ringleader in this persecution was Saul who hunted down Christians in a house-by-house search.

Instead of blocking the growth of the Christian movement, Luke reports "those who had been scattered preached the word wherever they went" (Acts 8:4). When Saul saw the church continuing to grow, he got permission from the Jewish high priest and set off for Damascus; he was intent on stamping out the Christian community which had sprung up there. On his way to Damascus Saul had an encounter with the living God; it completely changed his life. The Lord turned him around so that he joined the very people he had been pursuing. With the conversion of Saul the reign of terror came to an end.

Luke summarizes stage two: "Then the church throughout Judea, Galilee and Samaria enjoyed a time of peace. It was strengthened; and encouraged by the Holy Spirit, it grew in numbers, living in the fear of the Lord" (Acts 9:31).

3. *To the Gentiles (Acts 9:32—12:24).* A significant breakthrough occurs during this next phase. At first the movement had spread among the Jews and those not born Jewish but who had accepted and practiced the Jewish faith. Peter responded to an appeal from such a proselyte, Cornelius, a member of the Roman military, to explain the way of God more fully to him. The presence of the Holy Spirit in the life of Cornelius and his family shows that the gospel was intended for the Gentiles as much as for the Jews (Acts 11:17f.).

During the third stage, the church grew in a natural, unplanned way. As believers scattered in the wake of persecution, they shared their faith wherever they went (Acts 11:19). New congregations sprang up around these scattering witnesses.

Herod went on a rampage during this time, killing James and arresting Peter "when he saw that this pleased the Jews." Luke summarizes stage three: Despite the persecution "the word of God continued to increase and spread" (Acts 12:24).

4. *Sending Missionaries (Acts 12:25—16:5).* The next stage opens with a new way to carry forth the witness. Until this time the church had grown through the witness of believers as they fled persecution. Now, however, the church at Antioch was directed by the Holy Spirit to set apart Barnabas and Paul for a traveling ministry (Acts 13:1-3). The Antioch church commissioned Barnabas and Paul and sent them out on such a mission. As they evangelized in Cyprus and Asia Minor, they founded churches, appointing leaders for these new groups. They met repeated persecution and opposition.

After completing this missionary journey, Paul and Barnabas returned to Antioch. Here they "reported all that God had done through them and how he had opened the door of faith to the Gentiles" (Acts 14:27).

The growth of the Gentile church raised questions about standards for admission into the Christian faith. Was it necessary for converts to adopt Jewish ritual law or could Gentiles be accepted on the basis of their faith in Christ alone? In the great Jerusalem Conference Peter argued that the Holy Spirit was at work among the Gentiles just as had been true among the Jews. Therefore, it was not right to impose on the Gentiles rules and regulations out of the Jewish tradition. In the end the conference adopted this basic position (Acts 15).

Luke concludes this phase, saying: "So the churches were strengthened in the faith and grew daily in numbers" (Acts 16:5).

5. *To Far-off Lands (Acts 16:6—19:20).* During

this stage Paul undertook two more missionary journeys, extending the church in ever-widening circles as far west as Europe. From the outset of his missionary ministry Paul adopted the pattern of beginning his witness in a new community by going to the synagogue. There he would tell about Jesus and challenge his listeners to accept him as their promised Messiah.

Often this witness produced a sharp reaction. Some people would be persuaded, but others would reject Paul's teaching. Paul and his companions were often harassed, brought before magistrates, thrown into jail, or driven out of town.

But opposition did not stop Paul. He persisted in his witness. And God blessed his missionary work. Names such as Philippi, Athens, Corinth, and Ephesus are known as places Paul visited, leaving a body of believers behind in each.

Luke says about this stage: "In this way the word of the Lord spread widely and grew in power" (Acts 19:20).

6. *To Rome (Acts 19:21—28:30).* At the end of his third missionary journey Paul decided to pay another visit to Jerusalem. Along the way he visited some of the churches he had founded. Once in Jerusalem he met with the church leaders and reported on the further progress of the gospel.

But Paul had his enemies. Certain Jewish leaders turned a mob on Paul in the temple. This led to his arrest and imprisonment. When Paul demanded his rights as a Roman citizen, he was eventually sent to Rome to make his appeal to Caesar.

Luke's summary: "For two whole years Paul stayed there in his own rented house and welcomed all who came to see him. Boldly and without hindrance he preached the kingdom of God and taught about the Lord Jesus Christ" (Acts 28:30-31).

The Apostolic Message

Acts contains summaries of several sermons preached by Peter, Stephen, and Paul (Acts 2; 3:12-26; 7; 10:34-43; 13:16-41; 17:22-31). Most of these messages were given as a witness to those who had not yet accepted Jesus as Messiah. Paul wrote his epistles to groups in which both faith and unbelief clashed. Each sermon or epistle addressed a particular audience in terms they could understand. What is the core of the witness of the apostles and early missioners?

1. *Ephesians 2:11-22* pictures Messiah as the one who personally makes peace between individuals and groups alienated from one another. In the first section, 2:11, 12, the writer reminds the Ephesians that understanding begins with remembering. These Gentile believers were in danger of forgetting that they once lived under a fourfold handicap. They have been: (a) estranged from Jesus Christ, (b) alienated from God's people, Israel, (c) unaware of the covenants of promise, and (d) hopeless wanderers in the world. Their situation could only be described as desperate, wholly unsatisfactory. All humankind shares in this condition which produces hostility and separation among people.

Yet God refused to leave matters as they were (2:13-18). "But now in Christ Jesus" becomes the pivot for everything else. In this desperate human situation, only the shedding of the blood of Jesus Christ could open the way to reconciliation between humankind and God and between human beings. Paul uses a series of phrases to describe this peace-making action: "you . . . have been brought near," "he is our peace . . . made us both one . . . has broken down the dividing wall of hostility." The outcome is a new union. Jew and Gentile suddenly can stand on a common footing in a reconciled relationship of which peace is the hallmark.

All this is possible because Jesus Christ personally brings peace to all parties in the conflict—those who were "near" in covenant relationship to God and those who "were far off." The result of this work of Christ on our behalf is a new spiritual and social reality. Four new terms now characterize our position (2:19-22). We are: (a) fellow citizens, (b) members of God's household, (c) built on the foundation, and (d) part of God's temple. Thus the original situation is reversed. We who were dead are now alive.

2. *In 2 Corinthians* 5 Paul summarizes the human condition and God's provision for humankind.

Humanly speaking we live with a threefold awareness of ourselves (2 Corinthians 5:1-4). First, we all live with our mortality (v. 2). Our physical bodies become diseased, deteriorate with age, and die. Life is temporary.

Second, we long to transcend this physical body and be released into a perfect state (vv. 1-2). Images of Eden and exile come before us. The perfection of Eden, our rightful inheritance, may still be reclaimed.

Third, we live in anticipation of this change from mortality to eternal life (v. 4). Even those who do not know God as revealed in Jesus Christ share in these desires and longings. (see, for example, Acts 14:16, 17, Romans 1:19, 20; 2:12-16.)

This restlessness reflects God's Spirit at work in every life (2 Corinthians 5:5). When God made Adam and Eve they received God's breath (i.e., spirit). Because of sin, that spirit is restless until the sting of death is removed through faith in Christ. The presence of the Holy Spirit now in each believer is a guarantee that God will complete the work of redemption in those who submit themselves to God's rule. For the believer the Spirit's presence brings hope, confidence, and peace.

One thing is certain: All must appear before God, stripped of all pretense and the "figleaves" with which we each hide our shame (2 Corinthians 5:6-10). Those who have already received God's peace eagerly welcome this great climax. Those who have hidden their faces from God now find themselves unable to hide any longer.

Paul now puts forward two motives for sharing the gospel (2 Corinthians 5:11, 14). "Since, then, we know what it is to fear the Lord, we try to persuade men.... For Christ's love compels us...." The two motives—people's need to prepare to meet God and their love of Christ—are not in contradiction. The gospel faces every individual with the most important decision ever to be made: one's relationship with God who is both Creator and Redeemer. To approach God's judgment seat unprepared is a fearful prospect. But those who have already been saved and live in fellowship with God are controlled by Christ's love. That love restlessly seeks out those who have not met the divine love.

The work of Christ on our behalf gives a new

perspective on the human situation (2 Corinthians 5:16-21). All face death, but Christ died for all, thus putting death to flight. In Christ, death does not have the last word. Furthermore, Christ's sacrifice is universal. This means Christ's love reaches out to every human being. As we respond to that love and appropriate God's grace, we are transformed—restored to fellowship with God. The old death-bound life yields to the new. We are reconciled with our Creator/Redeemer. Once we are in union with Christ, he makes us his ministers of reconciliation, ambassadors of the King.

The Missionary Church: Moved by the Holy Spirit

For the people of Israel two root experiences formed their identity—exodus and Sinai. For the new Israel—the church—there is a new exodus and a new Sinai. The creation of the people of God under the new covenant hinges on two root experiences: the death and resurrection of Jesus the Messiah and Pentecost.

This is the age of the Holy Spirit. The work of the Holy Spirit is to witness to Jesus Christ. The apostles followed the guidance of the Holy Spirit when making each major decision or in taking a new direction in witness. The Holy Spirit has extended that witness throughout the world by sending the body of Christ, the church, into the world as heralds of the gospel.

The record of the early church is marked *not* by constant reference to a command to witness but by an inner force which compelled it to share that which it was experiencing. The apostle Paul exclaimed, "Woe to me if I do not preach the gospel!" (1 Corinthians 9:16b).

As we trace the development of the church, we note how the center of leadership and influence changes from one period to another. In the first years of the church it moved from Jerusalem to Antioch to Rome. Later the center moved to Western Europe. The dynamic center of the life of the church is always found where missionary consciousness is most acute. As the fires of church life ebb and the community settles into a routine, it loses its missionary passion. Then the center moves elsewhere.

Questions

1. What is the work of the Holy Spirit in mission?
2. List important factors in the rapid growth of the early church.
3. In what ways is the mission of your congregation related to human needs?
4. Does missionary expansion today have the same two-fold character—organic and apostolic—as that of the church in Acts?
5. Is Paul's description/definition of salvation in Ephesians 2 the one commonly used in your congregation? If not, why?

5

NINETEEN CENTURIES OF CHRISTIAN EXPANSION

THE story of the Christian faith is a story of small beginnings. Jesus appeared on the stage of history for a brief period of about three years. He gathered a small band of disciples around him and was killed at the early age of thirty-three. This man from Nazareth came from humble origins and had his greatest appeal among the lower classes. He rejected opportunities to gather political power to himself and preached a message which sounded strange to most of the people of his day. Such are the facts surrounding the origins of the movement which Jesus inspired nearly 2,000 years ago.

We want to trace briefly the history of that movement. What have been the changes in the character of the Christian faith over time? What have been the ebbs and flows in vitality?

Important Changes in the Faith

Changes in theology. In the beginning, Judaism cradled the faith Jesus lived and taught. The first Christians depended on the Jewish Bible—the Old Testament—as their Scriptures. They followed Jewish patterns of preaching and teaching. The early Christians continued to recite the stories of the history of salvation. They worshiped in the Jewish temple and synagogues. As Christians moved away from Palestine into other cultures, they faced new ideas about God, the world, and their place in it. For example, Christians encountered the Greeks who placed strong emphasis on human intelligence. In response to questions raised by Greek philosophies, Christians began to write systematic theologies and think in Greek patterns of thought.

Changes in planning. From the beginning, the movement of Jesus was carried on largely by the common people. Although a few apostles were specially commissioned to spread the faith, the local church was largely responsible for this work.

In A.D. 313, however, Emperor Constantine issued the Edict of Milan (also known as the Edict of Toleration) which made Christianity legally acceptable. Thereafter Christianity became the religion of the state, and the nature of the church and its methods were greatly affected. Missions to convert the heathen were commonly sponsored and supported by the state until the nineteenth century.

Monasteries were established as another means to

teach and spread the faith. Monastic priests were some of the most effective evangelists in bringing the gospel to Europe.

Other people became Christian through mass movements, when people accustomed to living as tight-knit groups made decisions collectively, not individually. Thus, throughout Christian history entire clans and tribes have become believers as a group rather than one-by-one.

Changes in impact. The Christian movement began among the people on the edge of society. The Jewish religious leaders and the Roman political leaders thought of Christians as a radical sect which threatened the security of established Judaism and state government.

Therefore, during the first generations the early Christians endured severe and persistent persecution. Many died as martyrs. By the fourth century after Christ, however, Christianity had been recognized as the official religion of the Roman Empire. This development radically changed the character of Christianity as well as the way Christians understood their calling to spread the gospel.

Ebbs and Flows

Throughout history the body of Christ has experienced periods of growth and expansion followed by periods of decline.*

First advance: From Pentecost to A.D. 500. Christianity took root in the Roman Empire when Roman power was at its peak. It began in the face of

---

*Statistics in this chapter are taken from David B. Barrett (ed.), *World Christian Encyclopedia* (Oxford, 1982).

great odds. Not only were believers persecuted by the state, but many other cults and religions also vied for the loyalties of the people.

Although the empire opposed Christianity, it also furnished channels for the spread of the faith. The world as a whole lived in peace during this time. The empire had developed an extensive system of roads and communications, and Christians freely followed these trade arteries, sharing their faith and forming congregations as they went.

Because the Roman Empire with its cultures was beginning to decay, Christian faith offered hope and new vitality. About A.D. 220 Origen wrote: "The gospel of Jesus Christ has been preached in all creation under heaven, to Greeks and barbarians, to wise and foolish . . . . It is impossible to see any race of men which has avoided accepting the teaching of Jesus."

But Origen also noted: "The gospel has not been preached to all nations, since it has not reached the Chinese or the Ethiopians beyond the river, and only small parts of the more remote and barbarous tribes." The awareness that some peoples had not yet heard the news about Jesus Christ impelled the church to continue the task of carrying the gospel to all the world.

By A.D. 500, 22 percent of the world's population had become Christian, according to estimates. These believers were scattered all around the Mediterranean basin. They were found from Mauritania along the Atlantic Ocean to the Arabian peninsula, from northern Europe to faraway Ceylon (now Sri Lanka). At least parts of the Christian Scriptures were available in thirteen languages.

First recession: 500-950. While the Christian movement had been gaining in strength and official acceptance, the Roman Empire had begun to decline. Repeated invasions from the north and northeast devastated the empire and threatened the church.

The church lost its spiritual power and soon became lifeless. Occasionally renewal movements touched the church, but these did not reawaken the church as a whole. External threats were equally damaging. Islam emerged in 622 and soon became a potent force as it sought to conquer and dominate. Wherever Islam gained control, Christianity went into eclipse.

Every period of advance carries within it the seeds of its decline, and each period of decline contains the seeds of renewal. Toward the end of the Dark Ages the church began to recover its inner strength. The pressure from Islam pushed the church into Europe where pagan tribes were open to the Christian message. Europe was to become the future stronghold of Christianity.

By 950 the number of Christians as a percentage of total population had declined to 19 percent. Muslims had swept across Palestine and Syria in 632. Jerusalem fell to Muslim invaders in 638. Islamic conquest continued in Egypt, Iraq, Spain, Portugal, and all of North Africa. Meanwhile, Christians advanced in Scandinavia and Eastern Europe while Nestorian missionaries extended their witness into various parts of Asia. But by 949, half of the territory under Christian influence had fallen to Islam.

The growing Europeanization of the church is reflected in the dramatic change in number of white to nonwhite adherents. In 500 this ratio is estimated to have been 62 percent nonwhite/38 percent white; in 950 the ratio had changed to 41 percent nonwhite/59 percent white.

Second advance: 950-1350. During the next three centuries Europe became the vital center for the Christian church. In 950 Christianity began to take root in Poland, Bulgaria, and Russia. The faith spread to Greenland in 990, and Hungary fell under Christian influence in 997. The last holdouts in Europe, the Prussians, were evangelized at that time. By 1000 Christian kingdoms were set up in Denmark, England, Hungary, Norway, Poland, Sweden, and Scotland. Iceland accepted Christianity in 1016—the only country to do so voluntarily and without political pressure.

Throughout this period conflict between the church and secular powers was intense. Successive popes struggled to free the church of secular control. They in turn acquired immense power which they did not hesitate to use to their advantage. One of the great blots on Christian history is the series of Crusades carried out between 1096 and 1291 with official encouragement from the popes. These military campaigns to take control of Palestine from the Muslims proved unsuccessful. To this day Middle Eastern peoples bear bitter memories of the Crusades.

Nevertheless the Christian movement grew rapidly during this era. The church had great influence on the development of European culture. Renewal movements, largely centered in the monasteries, helped reform corrupt practices and encouraged the spread of the gospel. The monks took up the large task of rooting the masses of nominal converts in the faith. In Europe the church played a dynamic role in all aspects of life. In contrast, the church in Muslim-controlled lands found itself choked and on the defensive. Outside of Europe and the Middle East Christians existed as pockets of believers.

Always some Christians protested against the use of force as a means of spreading the faith of Jesus Christ, but they remained a minority voice. The history of the church is marked by this fundamental compromise of the way of Jesus.

By 1350 Christians as a percentage of total population had risen again to about 24 percent, for the number of adherents in Europe increased rapidly. Christian Scriptures were available in twenty-eight languages.

Second recession: 1350-1500. As always, both external and internal forces caused the church to decline during this era. Externally, a rising Islam made inroads in Turkey and along the western shore of the Black Sea. Christianity was wiped out in China and lost out in Central Asia as well as Iran, Iraq, Upper Egypt, and Syria.

The Renaissance, a period of great interest in art and learning in Europe, introduced an attitude of skepticism. Since the church failed to come to grips with the Renaissance, much of Europe fell back into paganism. As the church's authority generally declined, it was beset by internal divisions. Church leaders were often corrupt and more interested in using their position for political than for spiritual purposes.

In this period of spiritual darkness, however, new

movements germinated and burst into new vitality. In 1500 Christians are thought to have accounted for 19 percent of total world population. More significantly, Europeans then accounted for the greater part of the total Christian population.

Third advance: 1500-1750. This period was marked by both reform and expansion. In 1500 the prospects for Christianity seemed bleak. The nations of Asia were more wealthy and culturally advanced than those of Europe, and Asian religions seemed more vigorous than did the Christianity of that age.

Early in the fifteenth century Portuguese explorers began making expeditions southward along the coast of Africa; Columbus crossed the Atlantic to the New World in 1492. This spirit of exploration remained a powerful force in Western cultural development for the next 300 years.

Because people had tired of the spiritual deadness and corruption of the church, they were eager for new life. Martin Luther's break with the Roman Catholic Church in 1517 was one part of this renewed Christianity. His protest against the state church system in Western Europe sparked a renewal that changed church history remarkably.

This Protestantism, as it came to be called, comprised several varieties: Lutherans, Calvinists, and Anabaptists. Of these three, only the Anabaptists began with a clear sense of the missionary nature of the church. They soon lost this mission consciousness, however, under the strain of persecution. The dominant varieties of Protestantism remained inactive as far as mission is concerned for 275 years.

Numerous renewal movements, however, remained loyal to the Roman Catholic Church. Old orders of priests experienced new vitality and became active in mission. Wherever Portuguese and Spanish explorers went, Catholic missionaries followed and the church took root. The link between state and mission was clear, for monarchs involved themselves directly in the sending of missionaries under royal support.

This period marks the first major step in the reshaping of Christian geography. Although Europe would remain the center of Christian life and action for another four centuries, the foundation for a strong church in the Americas, Asia, and Africa was being laid.

By 1750 the percentage of world population counted as Christian had climbed to 22 percent. The number of non-European Christians had increased somewhat, and the Scriptures were available in sixty languages.

Third recession: 1750-1815. During this period Christianity suffered some further losses of territory. It was almost snuffed out in Japan, China, and Paraguay. Indeed, the missions in all of Spanish America were discontinued around 1800. In Russia the church suffered from reversals in various places. Attempts to establish the church in Korea proved unsuccessful. During this time Spain and Portugal were in decline. They therefore were no longer able to give state support to the extensive network of missions which they had supported for so long. The Jesuits, who had been the main motor for Roman Catholic mission, lost favor with both government and the Roman Catholic hierarchy. Their order was dissolved by the pope in 1773. (In 1814 the Jesuits began again.) Various wars between the European powers and wars of revolution in the United States and France took their tolls.

Christianity was also declining in Europe. New ideas such as rationalism challenged the authority of religion, especially Christianity. The French revolution proved hostile to the church and put it on the defensive.

But there were also signs of renewal. A small group called the Moravians emerged in 1722, led by the dynamic Count Ludwig von Zinzendorf. He had a passion to win "souls for the Lamb." They sent their first missionaries in 1732 to the West Indies and the following year to Greenland. Although the Moravians never became a large group, they exerted immense influence by their example. They touched people such as John Wesley. He, along with his brother Charles and George Whitefield, spearheaded the Evangelical Revival in the British Isles and North America. This Revival did much to prepare the way for what has been called the "Great Century" in missions.

In 1815 Christians comprised 24 percent of world population. Scriptures by then were available in eighty-six languages.

Fourth advance: 1815-1914. The dates for this period are not exact, only a frame for discussion. The foundation for the Great Century was laid in the previous period. People such as William Carey of England had been agitating for some years to get support for missions. In 1792 Carey published his famous tract, *An Enquiry Into the Obligations of Christians to Use Means for the Conversion of the Heathens.* At the same time he pressured his friends into organizing the Particular Baptist Society for

Propagating the Gospel Among the Heathen (later the Baptist Missionary Society).

A flood of new mission organizations followed in the British Isles, Europe, and the United States. Whereas the Catholics had begun to retreat by about 1800, Protestants were just discovering their missionary obligation. They organized mission training schools, Bible societies, literature societies, and other mission-related activities. Then they began sending out missionaries.

This new wave of advance was assisted by the fact that the European powers were actively involved in exploration and extending their trading interests. Colonialism had already begun but would be greatly intensified by the emergence of the imperial spirit after 1850. Within a generation the Europeans would control the entire world.

The outcome of this unprecedented burst of missionary activity is told, in part, by the statistics on the eve of World War I. The number of Christians in the world by then represented almost 35 percent of world population. The proportion of non-Europeans had increased substantially, and at least some Scriptures were available in 676 languages.

Fourth recession: 1914-1950. Throughout most of the Great Century the British dominated Protestant missions. After 1910 the Americans surpassed the British in both the number of workers and finances.

World War I put a brake on missions. German missions suffered the worst disruption, but all European missions had an increasingly difficult time during and following the war. A decrease in the amount of money available was only a part of the reason for this slowdown. The growing spirit of nationalism among the colonized peoples of Asia and Africa bred unrest. Churches founded by missions were caught up in this movement too. In both church and nation these peoples wished to be free of outside domination. The mission-founded churches sensed increasingly the challenge of putting down roots in local soil. Otherwise, their witness would seem invalid and merely the promoting of a Western religion.

In Europe the churches were losing ground as antireligious philosophies gained influence. As people gave more attention to worldly matters, support for mission declined.

Before the world had recovered fully from the first World War a second one broke out. World War II foretold the end of colonialism and colonial missions. When the war ended in 1945 it was no longer a question *if* but *when* the colonies would be granted full independence. The churches also wanted independence from missions.

The nineteenth and twentieth centuries have brought changes in technology unknown before in history. When William Carey went to India in 1793, an exchange of letters between him and his Society in England took a full six months. Vastly changed transportation and communication systems have brought distant parts of the world closer together. At the same time the Christian church spread into nearly every country of the world. By 1950 a new appreciation for the *ecúmene*, the worldwide body of Christ, was being felt by all Christians.

In 1950 Christians as a percentage of world population had dropped to just over 34 percent and the non-European proportion had increased to 37 percent. Portions of the Scriptures had been published in 1,052 languages.

Fifth advance: 1950-1980. Following World War I the United States became dominant in world affairs. The center of Christian initiative had also passed from European to American hands about the same time.

Following World War II missionary activity began to surge again. Many new, nondenominational agencies sprang up to carry out a variety of ministries. The newly independent nations of Asia and Africa were calling for assistance in nation-building. Although missions had traditionally been concerned with the whole person—building hospitals and schools as well as churches—this drive toward nationhood was urgent. The new thrust centered on economic and community development.

The age of geographical exploration had come to an end by 1900. The notion of geographical frontiers ceased to have the same significance for missions as it had had earlier. New kinds of frontiers emerged. Political and economic systems have now divided the world into blocs. Marxism has become the ideological basis for governing a major portion of the world's peoples. Its anti-God, antireligion bias, when translated into official policy, has placed many Christians in a difficult position. Some estimates are that more Christians have died as martyrs in the twentieth century than in all previous centuries.

This latest period of missionary advance has produced a significant shift in the Christian world. Christianity in the West continues to lose members at the rate of some 1,820,000 per year. Whereas the Christian population grew at the rate of 1.2 percent during the Great Century, since 1950 Christianity has been losing at the rate of one percent per decade. Were it not for the continued rapid growth in Africa, Latin America, and Asia, the future of Christianity would look quite bleak.

The center of influence for the Christian world is shifting from the North to the South. Latin America is the largest Roman Catholic continent. Africa will shortly be the largest continent in terms of total Christian adherents. The church worldwide continues to grow most rapidly among the poor and oppressed. They are the ones who hear in the message of Jesus words of hope and the promise of new life.

Questions

1. Summarize and compare the reasons for growth during periods of advance and for decline during periods of recession.
2. Do you see parallels between these earlier periods and the situation today? Where would you place your church: in a period of advance or of recession?
3. What role have renewal movements played in new advance?
4. What impact, if any, have martyrdoms in the twentieth century had on the character of Christian faith (a) in the countries of the martyrs and (b) in the West?

GLOBAL STATUS OF CHRISTIANITY

(at end of historical epochs)

Year	*Christians as percentage of total population*	*Non-White/ White breakdown*	*Languages in which Scriptures are available*
500	22.4%	61.9/38.1%	13
950	19.0	41.2/58.8	17
1350	24.1	32.4/67.6	28
1500	19.0	7.4/92.6	12
1750	22.2	14.8/85.2	60
1815	24.4	13.9/86.1	86
1914	34.9	23.8/76.2	676
1950	34.1	36.5/63.5	1,052
1980	32.8	49.5/50.5	1,811

From *World Christian Encyclopedia*

WORLD POPULATION

Year	*Total Population (millions)*	*Christian Population (millions)*
33	169.7	0.0
500	193.4	43.4
1000	269.2	50.4
1350	359.7	86.7
1500	425.3	81.0
1750	720.7	160.0
1800	902.6	208.2
1900	1,619.9	558.1
1950	2,510.0	855.9
1980	4,373.9	1,432.7
2000	6,259.6 (est.)	2,019.9 (est.)

From *World Christian Encyclopedia*

THE GROWTH OF CHRISTIANITY, A.D. 33-1980

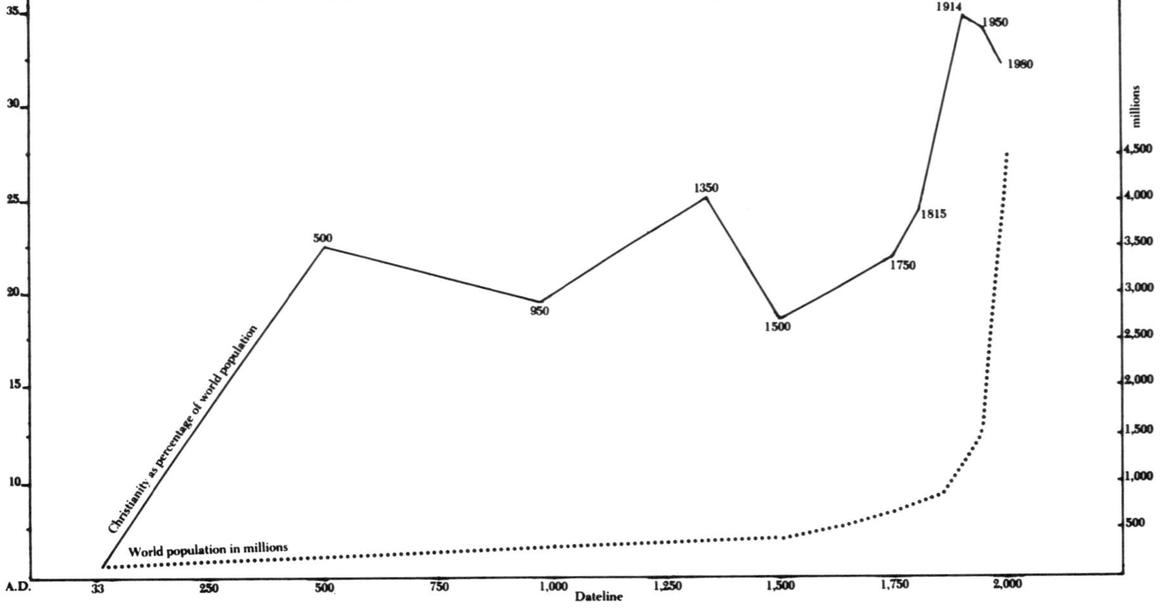

6

A MISSIONARY CHURCH

THREE observations stand out from our study of the church in Acts and in history since then. We will consider each of these obervations briefly.

Observation 1: The center of Christian life and action has moved repeatedly—from Jerusalem and Antioch to Rome; from Rome to Western Europe; and from Europe to North America. Why?

Part of the answer seems to be that the church flourishes where there are Christian resources. In the first days of the movement, the leadership and most members were to be found near Jerusalem and, soon thereafter, Antioch. Strong persons emerged who provided good leadership.

On the other hand, we also notice that the Christian faith has moved to the centers of power and influence. Some Christians, such as the apostle Paul, went to Rome as prisoners. Others moved there voluntarily as they followed commercial opportunities or political and social interests.

The center has also shifted to where the church has remembered its mission clearly. Where the church must struggle against fierce opposition or becomes too much like the world around it, it loses sight of its purpose.

The church's understanding of its mission needs to be challenged and purified by the gospel. When a worldly spirit or method motivates the church, it may appear to be moving forward. The results, however, may not be in the spirit of the gospel. At the heart of mission must be the clear awareness of the struggle between Christ and anti-Christ, a struggle which can be won only at the cross. Several years ago an Asian Christian remarked: "The trouble with Christians in the West is that they no longer realize there is a boundary between the two kingdoms. We in Africa and Asia cannot forget this for a moment." Mission must participate in this struggle between the kingdom of God and the kingdom of the world.

Observation 2: The New Testament describes two main patterns of expansion. The first pattern we may call organic or natural growth. Acts 11:19-26 pictures the first Christians being scattered by persecution following the martyrdom of Stephen. We do not meet these people by name, but Luke notes: "The Lord's hand was with them, and a great number of people believed and turned to the Lord" (v. 21). These rank-and-file members were faithful in witness wherever they went, producing new bodies of believers.

Acts 13:1-4a introduces the second pattern. Some specially gifted individuals were called by the Spirit and commissioned by the church for a traveling ministry to new areas. Paul and Barnabas formed the first such apostolic team. Of these two patterns by far the greater amount of work has been done by many unnamed witnesses. Neither of these two approaches—natural or planned growth—is complete without the other. Many times traveling evangelists have served as an advance party prepares the way. They laid the foundation, and others built on it by taking the witness to the many places not reached initially.

Observation 3: The congregation is the basic unit for mission. The Antioch church illustrates this. We have already noted how scattering Christians carried out a vigorous witness in the Antioch region. But the Antioch church also allowed the Holy Spirit to call Barnabas and Paul away for an apostolic ministry. When they completed their first missionary journey they returned to Antioch to report to the church (Acts 14:26f.).

We need to evaluate carefully the organization and self-understanding of each of our congregations. Does it conceive of itself as being a mission and does its structure serve mission? Or does its structure make the stranger feel unwelcome, as though the church were an exclusive club? Wherever the Christian movement is becoming weak and forgetting its reason for existence, congregations must learn again their mission and organize so they can best carry it out.

Recovery of Mission Consciousness

The church may continue to exist as a religious group in society long after it has lost its sense of purpose. It may still have the outward forms but lack spiritual reality. The church which is alive in the Spirit of God is sure to have a strong sense of mission. How does the church which has lost this purpose recover it? This will involve the recovery of vision and motivation.

1. *The Great Commission defines the church's task* as making disciples and nurturing them in the faith. But it makes this task a worldwide one. Every church is called to make disciples in its local community, in the region around, in the nation, and in the nations. The Great Commission forces us to face outward, beyond the concerns and welfare of our own congregation. The church which neglects this commissioning of Christ will soon lose its sense of mission. With this biblical understanding we can never say the evangelistic task is finished or that any people are fully Christian. Every generation must be won, and only some of the peoples of the world have heard of Jesus Christ.

2. *Pentecost provides power for mission.* No true mission exists until the Holy Spirit empowers for mission. The history of the church is full of instances where individuals or groups have carried out missions using means that turned the gospel into bad news. Too often the church has seen little fruitfulness in witness. Jesus instructed the disciples to *wait* until he sent the Holy Spirit to them. The Spirit is the true leader in mission. When the church submits to the Spirit's leadership it receives a sharpened awareness that mission is urgent and important.

Mission and Nurture

Every congregation must find a healthy balance between *mission* and *nurture*, between its responsibility to the world and its responsibility to its members. The following diagram represents this relationship.

Figure 1

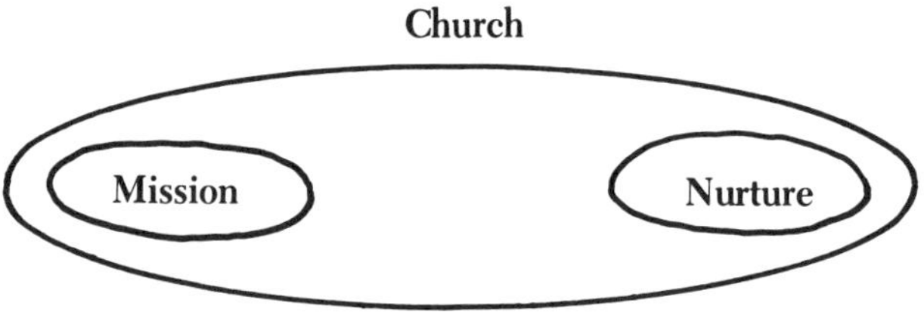

This calls for a biblical vision of both church and world. In God's plan the church has a special responsibility for the world. God created the world and has never given up claim to it. But the world is in bondage to evil. God has called the church to be the instrument through which he seeks to reclaim the world and restore it to its original purposes. The church must constantly remind itself of this responsibility to the world even though the world opposes and mistreats it.

Some churches, however, emphasize mission to the neglect of nurture of their own members. This imbalance produces a church which has little depth because it constantly emphasizes the winning of new people but fails to take the time to ground them in the faith. Gradually it loses its vitality. The following diagram illustrates this neglect.

Figure 2

Church

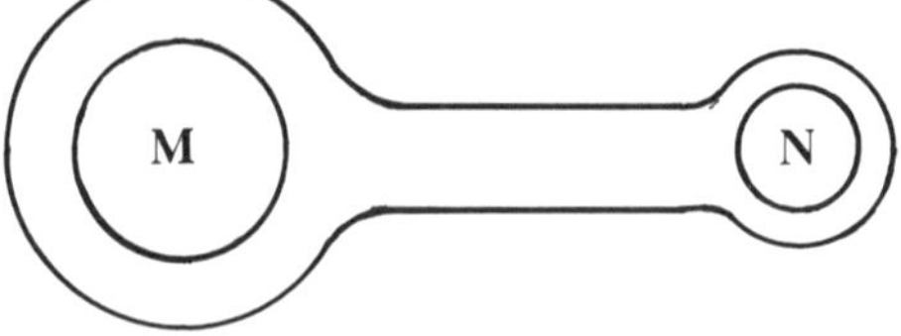

Other churches put nurture first. They protect and pamper their members in the name of nurture, as this diagram shows.

Figure 3

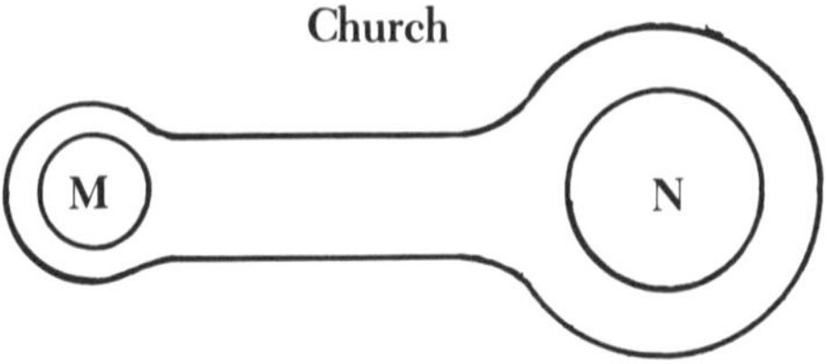

This emphasis produces a church preoccupied with self and dedicated to self-preservation. Such a church loses its missionary concern.

True missionary concern will result in people coming to faith in Jesus as Lord. True nurture builds up the new believers in the faith but must have as its final goal equipping them for ministry and witness. In other words, true nurture produces a fresh group of witnesses to the world.

Nurture which aims only at preparing people for heaven is not biblical. Biblical nurture prepares one for Christian service. We will be judged by how faithfully we ministered with the gift we received. In the biblical view nurture cannot be separated from mission. Mission must be undergirded by nurture if it is to avoid becoming superficial and ineffective; nurture must have mission as its ultimate outcome.

A Practical Exercise

What kind of congregation do I belong to? Is it a congregation with a strong mission awareness growing out of its faith? Or is it preoccupied with nurture and maintaining its own life?

One way to gain a clearer understanding of a congregation is to tell its history as mission history. In telling this story as mission history, we will want to find out when mission awareness was most evident.

What were the signs of such vitality?

When the congregation was preoccupied with internal concerns, what themes were prominent?

Who are the individuals who played a role in stimulating mission vision, and how did they do it?

What forces worked against this sense of mission?

How long did the congregation sustain a strong mission commitment?

How did the congregation change its patterns of life and witness as it became missionary?

How did members of the congregation understand their community, and in what ways did they reach out to the community?

Assuming that no congregation can sustain the same level of mission vitality at all times, trace the ebbs and flows. Note the differences in the quality of congregational life during these various periods.

After you have answered the above questions, how would you describe your congregational life to fellow members? Do you recommend planning a new course or continuing on your present path? How would you redesign your congregation's organization and pattern of life to make it a truly missionary church?

Renew Your Church, O God

The story of salvation centers on God choosing a people who will be the means of blessing for the whole world. The people of God, as we have noted, frequently failed. Yet the burden of responsibility has not been lifted; it rests directly on each local congregation to be witnesses within the community. Witness to the good news is intended to be given within relationships of love, integrity, and respect. In each generation the church needs to be renewed by the Holy Spirit for its task of witnessing to Jesus Christ who saves and reigns in the life of his people.

The last word in any missionary endeavor will be a word of praise and adoration: "For from him and through him and to him are all things. To him be the glory forever! Amen" (Romans 11:36).

FOR FURTHER STUDY

Barrett, David B. (ed). *World Christian Encyclopedia.* New York: Oxford, 1982.

Bosch, David J. *Witness to the World.* Atlanta: John Knox, 1980.

DeRidder, Richard. *Discipling the Nations.* Grand Rapids: Baker, 1975.

Dyrness, William. *Let the Earth Rejoice!* Westchester: Crossway, 1983.

Graber, J. D. *The Church Apostolic.* Scottdale: Herald Press, 1960.

Jacobs, Donald R. *Pilgrimage in Mission.* Scottdale: Herald Press, 1983.

Kraus, C. Norman. *The Authentic Witness.* Grand Rapids: Eerdmans, 1979.

__________. *The Community of the Spirit*. Grand Rapids: Eerdmans, 1974.
Kraus, C. Norman (ed). *Missions, Evangelism and Church Growth*. Scottdale: Herald Press, 1980.
Ramseyer, Robert L. (ed). *Mission and the Peace Witness*. Scottdale: Herald Press, 1979.
Shenk, Wilbert R. (ed). *Anabaptism and Mission*. Scottdale: Herald Press, 1984.
__________. *Exploring Church Growth*. Grand Rapids: Eerdmans, 1983.
__________ *Mission Focus: Current Issues*. Scottdale: Herald Press, 1980.

Wilbert R. Shenk is vice-president of Overseas Ministries for Mennonite Board of Missions, Elkhart, Indiana, and a member of the Belmont Mennonite Church, also in Elkhart. He also gives leadership to mission thought, planning, and practice for the Mennonite Church.

Wilbert studied at Goshen College (BA), at the University of Oregon (MA), and at the University of Aberdeen (PhD). Much of his study and life has centered on the mission of the church. Among the committees on which he serves or has served are: Mennonite Central Committee, the Institute of Mennonite Studies, the Council of International Ministries, and the American Society of Missiology.

He has written or edited a number of articles and publications, including: *The Challenge of Church Growth—A Symposium* (Herald Press, 1973), *Mission*

Focus: Current Issues (Herald Press, 1980), *Henry Venn—Missionary Statesman* (Orbis, 1983), *Exploring Church Growth* (Eerdmans, 1983), and *Anabaptism and Mission* (Herald Press, 1984). He is editor of *Mission Focus,* an inter-Mennonite quarterly journal published by MBM to deal with themes concerning the mission of the church.

His experience includes serving with Mennonite Central Committee in Indonesia (1955-59), as assistant director of Overseas Service for MCC (1963-65), as assistant secretary of Overseas Missions for MBM (1965-67), and as secretary of Overseas Missions for MBM (1967-80) until he was named to his current post with MBM.

Wilbert and his wife, Juanita, are the parents of Suzanne, Maria, and Thomas. They live in Elkhart, Indiana.

MENNONITE FAITH SERIES

Edited by
Elizabeth Showalter and *J. Allen Brubaker*

This series of books sets forth briefly and simply some of the major emphases of the New Testament as understood in the Anabaptist-Mennonite tradition—a faith which represents a cluster of emphases somewhat in contrast with those of the major bodies of Christendom in the sixteenth century: Roman Catholic, Orthodox, Anglican, Lutheran, and Reformed.

1. *How Mennonites Came to Be* by J. C. Wenger
2. *What Mennonites Believe* by J. C. Wenger
3. *The Way to a New Life* by J. C. Wenger
4. *The Way of Peace* by J. C. Wenger
5. *Disciples of Jesus* by J. C. Wenger
6. *The Way of True Riches* by Milo Kauffman
7. *Teaching in the Congregation* by Paul M. Lederach
8. *The Book We Call the Bible* by J. C. Wenger
9. *A Faith to Live By* by J. C. Wenger
10. *The Family of Faith* by J. C. Wenger
11. *The Way of Biblical Justice* by José Gallardo
12. *Evangelism as Discipling* by Myron S. Augsburger
13. *What We Believe About Children* by Marvin K. Yoder
14. *Some People Are Throwing You into Confusion* by Pierre Widmer
15. *The Church in Mission* by Wilbert R. Shenk

The books in this series are published in North America by:

HERALD PRESS
616 Walnut Avenue
Scottdale, Pa. 15683

HERALD PRESS
117 King Street, West
Kitchener, Ont. N2G 4M5

Overseas persons wanting copies of the booklets or permission to translate should write to: Mennonite Board of Missions, 1251 Virginia Ave., Harrisonburg, Va. 22801.